T0414016

From our humble beginnings as a fledgling startup to our current status as a growth-stage company with seven-figure revenues, this book tells the story of our incredible ascent at Streann Media. It's a tale highlighted by the significant contributions of visionary investors, the dedication of our amazing, distributed team across the globe, and the relentless drive of our founders who never gave up. Together, we have navigated the complexities of the digital age, pioneered innovative solutions, and built strong relationships with our customers, reshaping the streaming landscape. Dive into our journey as we share the innovative spirit, strategic insights, and unwavering commitment to excellence that have been the hallmarks of our success. "Unstoppable Rise" is more than just our history—it's a beacon for all entrepreneurs, filled with lessons on collaboration, innovation, and the power of a shared vision. Join us in celebrating our past and inspiring the future.

Gio Punzo & Antonio Calderon

SHARE YOUR STORY;
THE WORLD IS WAITING FOR YOU!

EACH ONE OF US HAS A UNIQUE JOURNEY FILLED WITH STORIES THAT HAVE THE POWER TO INSPIRE, EDUCATE, AND ENTERTAIN. WHAT'S THE STORY YOU WANT TO TELL? THE WORLD IS NOT JUST WAITING; IT'S EAGER TO WATCH AND LISTEN.

"DO WHAT YOU DO WITH LOVE, SHARE IT WITH THE WORLD, CONNECT WITH HEARTS, AND SUCCESS WILL FOLLOW.

FIGURING OUT WHAT YOUR ADVENTURE IS ALL ABOUT!—ITS VISION, PURPOSE, AND KEY AREAS OF FOCUS—IS CRUCIAL. AT STREANN, WE'VE BUILT OUR JOURNEY AROUND FOUR PILLARS: CONTENT, DISTRIBUTION, ENGAGEMENT, AND MONETIZATION.

These foundations guide our growth and every solution we bring to the market. Identifying your company's pillars early on will illuminate your path, ensuring every step is purpose-driven and aligned with your mission. Remember, the stronger your base, the higher you can climb!

ENGAGEMENT

= MONETIZATION

"TOGETHER, WE ADAPT AND THRIVE.

WHEN COVID-19 HIT THE WORLD, IT CHALLENGED US ALL. THIS GLOBAL EPIDEMIC TAUGHT US A SECRET POWER: RESILIENCE. BEING READY TO CHANGE AND TRY NEW THINGS IS LIKE HAVING A MAGIC SHIELD. IT HELPS US KEEP GOING AND GROWING, NO MATTER WHAT.

While we witnessed businesses around the globe shutting down. We worked together, even though we were in different places, like a puzzle fitting perfectly. This resilience helped us keep moving forward. We discovered it's super important to quickly think of new ideas and make sure what we do fits what our customers need.

"DIVE INTO THE DIGITAL WORLD, WHERE IMAGINATION IS YOUR PLAYGROUND AND INNOVATION LEADS THE WAY TO NEW REALITIES.

STUDY THE MARKET, LOOK FOR TRENDS. BY ALWAYS ADDING THE COOLEST AND MOST INNOVATIVE STUFF TO WHAT WE OFFER, WE STAND OUT AS LEADERS.

IT'S LIKE BEING IN A SUPER FUN RACE WHERE WE'RE NOT JUST RUNNING ALONG WITH EVERYONE ELSE, BUT SPRINTING AHEAD, SUPER FAST! THIS WAY, WE STAY IN THE LEAD AND BECOME A TEAM THAT EVERYONE ELSE ADMIRES AND WANTS TO BE LIKE."

ACROSS OUR HUGE, WONDERFUL WORLD,
OUR TEAM IS GROWING!

WE'RE FINDING SMART, CREATIVE STREANNERS FROM ALL THE DIFFERENT PLACES YOU CAN POINT TO ON A MAP.

WE'RE LIKE A TEAM OF SUPERHEROES, CONNECTED DIGITALLY, WORKING TOGETHER NO MATTER HOW MANY MILES ARE BETWEEN US. IT'S LIKE WE HAVE A MAGIC NET THAT LETS US CATCH THE BRIGHTEST STARS FROM ANYWHERE, AND TOGETHER, WE SHINE LIKE A SUPER MACHINE, MAKING EVERYTHING BETTER, MORE FUN AND CHANGING THE WORLD TOGETHER!"

Dream big and believe in the mission.

Every award is a clear sign of our leadership and team's dedication.

It's a sign, telling us and the world that we're on the right track, and all the hard work is really making a difference.

Let this inspire you: when teamwork, passion, and persistence align, recognition and success will naturally follow.

REVOLUTIONIZING THE WAY WE CONNECT, THE NEW ERA OF TELEVISION, ENTERTAINMENT BRINGS STORIES TO LIFE, INTERACTIVE EXPERIENCES WITH ENDLESS POSSIBILITIES.

TAKE THE TIME TO PAUSE, TAKE A STEP BACK, AND LOOK AT THE BIG PICTURE TO FIND THE MISSING PIECES OF THE PUZZLE.

LISTENING IS AN ART, TEAM BRAINSTORMING SESSIONS BREATHE NEW LIFE INTO OUR SERVICES, DRIVING ITS EVOLUTION TO MEET OUR END USERS' NEEDS FOR FRESH FEATURES. WE'RE COMMITTED TO CONNECTING HEARTS AND SCREENS, CREATING EXPERIENCES THAT DEEPLY TOUCH OUR AUDIENCE

SURE, YOU'LL RUN INTO CHALLENGES ON YOUR WAY TO SUCCESS,
BUT THAT'S JUST PART OF THE ADVENTURE. IT'S ALL ABOUT FACING
THOSE CHALLENGES HEAD-ON AND FINDING YOUR PATH TO YOUR
BIGGEST DREAMS. JUST LIKE ASTRONAUTS EXPLORING SPACE, WE'RE
TAKING OUR DREAMS WORLDWIDE. REMEMBER, YOU'RE CAPABLE OF
REACHING THE STARS IF YOU'RE DETERMINED TO FIND A WAY.

Together, we spell 'FUTURE', and that's what we're all about at Streann.

We're a team, like a family, that builds cool technology to tell stories, that make people smile. Every day, we're inventors and explorers, finding new ways to bring joy and

LEARNING TO KIDS AND GROWN-UPS EVERYWHERE. AND REMEMBER, EVERY BIG IDEA STARTS WITH A DREAM, SO KEEP DREAMING AND CREATING, BECAUSE YOU'RE PART OF THIS EXCITING JOURNEY INTO TOMORROW TOO.

AS ENTREPRENEURS, WE DON'T HAVE A 'PLAN B' BECAUSE OUR HEARTS ARE SET ON 'PLAN A'—THE BIG DREAM.

WE KEEP OUR TEAM UNITED, EVEN IF WE'RE SPREAD OUT LIKE A CONSTELLATION ACROSS THE SKY, BELIEVING IN THE BIG PICTURE

THAT GUIDES US. TOGETHER, WE'RE CREATING A FUTURE THAT'S AS BRIGHT AND CONNECTED AS WE ARE, SHOWING THE WORLD JUST WHAT CAN HAPPEN WHEN YOU HOLD ON TO YOUR DREAMS AND WORK AS ONE.

THIS IS JUST THE BEGINNING!

WITH ARTIFICIAL INTELLIGENCE, AUGMENTED REALITY, APPLE VISION PRO, SMART TVS, AND LIVE STREAMING ON SOCIAL MEDIA, GET READY FOR A WHOLE NEW WORLD OF ENTERTAINMENT EXPERIENCES. WE'RE LEADING THE WAY, REWRITING THE RULES, AND BRINGING PEOPLE TOGETHER THROUGH THE MAGIC OF SCREENS, BECAUSE WE ARE EXPERTS AND LOVE WHAT WE DO. AND REMEMBER, WHEN YOU DO WHAT YOU LOVE, THE BEST IS YET TO COME!"

DID YOU KNOW? SUCCESS DOESN'T HAPPEN OVERNIGHT!

IT TOOK US YEARS TO GET WHERE WE ARE TODAY. WE'VE BEEN
GROWING, WORKING HARD, AND ALWAYS FINDING NEW WAYS TO MAKE

THINGS BETTER. IT'S ALL ABOUT LEARNING TO GROW, AND NEVER
GIVING UP! SOMETIMES, NOT EVERYONE SEES WHAT YOU SEE, AND
THAT'S OKAY. WE HAVE A SAYING: 'IF WE RECEIVE A NO, THANK YOU,
NEXT, IT MEANS THEY ARE NOT READY'

BEING REJECTED ONLY MAKES US STRONGER. WE'VE SHARED OUR STORY IN ALMOST 1000 PITCHES AND NOW WE HAVE THOUSANDS OF CUSTOMERS AND MILLIONS OF USERS WHO ARE BENEFITING FROM OUR INVENTIONS IN 141 GEOGRAPHIES!

DON'T STOP BELIEVING!

"TELL YOUR STORY LOUD AND CLEAR, AND ALWAYS KEEP YOUR EYES ON THE MISSION!

JOIN THE COMMUNITY AND FORM NEW PARTNERSHIPS THAT CAN HELP YOUR BUSINESS GROW. WE BUILT STREANN UNIVERSITY TO TEACH OUR TEAM AND CUSTOMERS ALL ABOUT OUR TECHNOLOGY. WE'VE TAKEN PART IN AWARDS PROGRAMS, SHOWCASED OUR INNOVATIONS IN ACCELERATORS AND TRADE SHOWS, AND JOINED LOCAL EVENTS TO SPREAD THE WORD, WIN AWARDS, AND SHARE OUR JOURNEY WITH OUR COMMUNITY.

TV 3.0 REPRESENTS THE NEXT WAVE OF ENTERTAINMENT, BLENDING AI, AR, AND SOCIAL CONTENT PLATFORMS.

NOT EVERYONE WILL ENVISION THIS, AND AS AN ENTREPRENEUR

IT'S YOUR DUTY TO LEAD THE PATH. EARLY ADOPTERS WILL DIVE IN
HEADFIRST AND BECOME PIONEERS OF THIS NEW ERA. AS YOU AND
YOUR TEAM GROW, TAKE A MOMENT TO REFLECT, REVIEW YOUR
ROADMAP, MAKE TWEAKS, LISTEN, AND GO FOR IT AT FULL SPEED,

As you grow, you have a social responsibility to your customers, your partners and your family!

Just like in soccer, where teamwork is everything, growing your startup means playing together for your partners and investors.

You're not on the field alone, and every move you make is part of a bigger game plan.
When you score a goal by showing good results, your whole team — investors included — will cheer for you!

GETTING A PATENT IS LIKE WINNING A PRIZE THAT SAYS YOUR IDEA IS SUPER-ORIGINAL!

THINK OF A PATENT AS A GOLDEN TICKET THAT SAYS YOUR IDEA IS TOTALLY UNIQUE, LIKE A ONE-OF-A-KIND TOY THAT NO ONE ELSE HAS EVER THOUGHT OF. WE GOT THIS GOLDEN TICKET FOR OUR INVENTION, BUT WOW, IT WASN'T EASY! JUST LIKE WHEN YOU'RE

LEARNING TO RIDE A BIKE AND YOU KEEP FALLING OFF, WE HEARD 'NO' A LOT. BUT WE KEPT TRYING AND TRYING, BECAUSE GETTING YOUR IDEA PATENTED IS LIKE GETTING A SUPERHERO'S BADGE THAT SAYS YOUR IDEA IS SUPER SPECIAL.

Social media is the new Media.

Remember to use it to spread goodness, learn new things, and share your own amazing story. But don't forget, it's not the only book on the shelf! Always ask questions and use it wisely, like a tool in your adventure kit that helps you discover even more of the world!

We've started to add social media features into our products around the pillars of Content, Engagement,

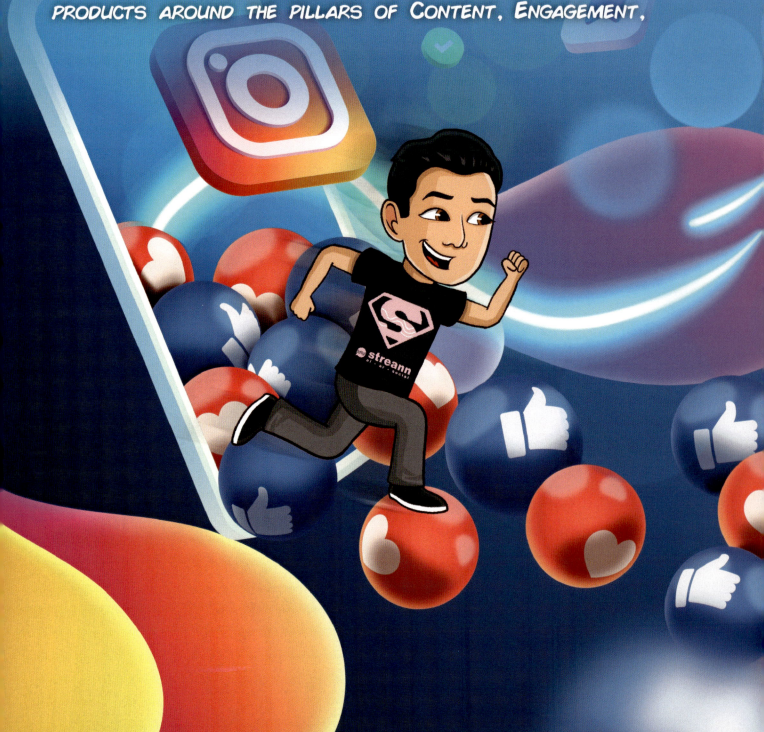

MONETIZATION ALLOWING OUR CUSTOMERS TO DO GOOD, ENABLING THEIR END USERS TO CREATE STORIES, COMPETE AGAINST THE NEW MEDIA, MONETIZING WITH MICROPAYMENTS AND START A REVOLUTION THAT WE CALL TV 3.0.

IMAGINE SOCIAL MEDIA FOR EDUCATION, FOR WOMEN, FOR FAITH, FOR SPORTS, AND SO ON."

THERE'S NO SUCH THING AS FAILING,
ONLY LEARNING AND GROWING!

THINK BACK TO THE FOUR PILLARS WE MENTIONED. NOT EVERYTHING
FEATURE WE MAKE WILL BE A HIT, BUT IF WE DON'T GIVE IT A
GO, WE'LL NEVER FIND OUT. IT'S IMPORTANT TO DO YOUR

HOMEWORK, HEAR WHAT PEOPLE NEED, WATCH WHAT'S POPULAR, AND THEN DIVE IN.

EVERY OOPSIE IS JUST A STEP TO GETTING SMARTER, A CLUE FOR WHAT TO DO BETTER NEXT TIME.

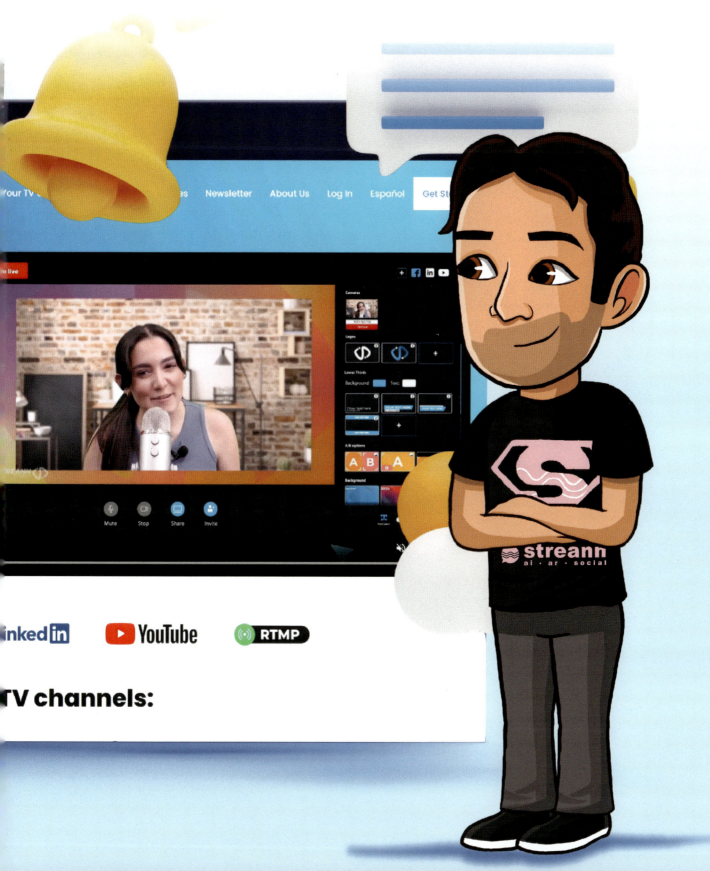

UNDERSTAND WHAT YOU'RE GREAT AT AND MAKE THE MOST OF YOUR TALENTS.

REMEMBER, IN A TEAM, EVERYONE HAS THEIR OWN SUPERPOWERS. KNOWING WHAT YOUR SUPERPOWERS ARE IS WHAT MAKES YOU

INCREDIBLE. WHETHER YOU'RE WRITING ABOUT COOL NEW PRODUCTS DOCUMENTATION OR PUTTING TOGETHER EXCITING GAME SHOWS FOR SOCIAL MEDIA MARKETING, USE YOUR STRENGTHS TO SHINE AND SHOW EVERYONE THE AMAZING THINGS YOU CAN DO!

Honesty and transparency are the bricks that build our team's tower of success!

Whether you're cozy at home or having fun at the office, having an open space in your mind helps everyone talk and share ideas better. It's like being on a team, where trust, sticking to your tasks, and being honest are super important.

THIS NEW WAY WE WORK, SOMETIMES AT HOME, SOMETIMES AT THE OFFICE, IS LIKE A GAME WHERE WE LEARN TO STAY FOCUSED AND DO OUR BEST. THE LEADERS ARE LIKE COACHES, MAKING SURE EVERYONE CAN BE A STAR PLAYER, AND GUESS WHAT? IT REALLY WORKS!"

As we conclude this volume on Streann Media's evolution, we stand poised to embrace an ambitious new phase. The leap from startup to industry leader was just the beginning. Now, we prepare to delve deeper and reach further.

Our next book will outline the pioneering strategies set to drive our growth—expanding internationally, integrating cutting-edge AI to refine content delivery, and prioritizing sustainability and community impact to enrich our corporate ethos.

Embark with us on this exciting journey as we navigate the uncharted territories of the digital landscape. Together, we'll unlock new opportunities and redefine what it means to lead in the streaming space.

Thank you for sharing in our story thus far. We look forward to exploring this new chapter with you, where innovation meets impact, and every stream weaves a richer narrative. Let's continue to innovate and inspire, creating a legacy that lasts.

Gio Punzo & Antonio Calderon